S0-AUZ-258

FUN·TO·LEARN
SCIENCE

Arianne Holden

Educational Consultant: Sharon Whittingham

LORENZ BOOKS

NOTES

Fun to Learn Science introduces children to essential science concepts in a lively and stimulating way that is guaranteed to capture their imagination.

Learning the basics
This book shows children that science is part of their everyday lives, as they throw a ball, push a truck or whizz down a slide. There are plenty of simple experiments and investigations that will strengthen children's understanding and encourage them to find out even more.

Reading together
Most children benefit from adult help when reading a book. Do not expect a child to grasp all the information at once! It is better to look at one concept at a time and allow a few days for the information to be absorbed.

Talking it through
Talk about the things you have found out together. Make everyday activities into a science adventure—bathtime is perfect for talking about floating and sinking, or hot and cold, and preparing dinner is a chance to think about melting, heating and how cooking something can change it.

Answering questions
Ask your child questions and encourage him or her to answer. Do not worry if the answers are wrong—making mistakes is part of the learning process. The most important thing is that your child feels confident and willing to try.

Checking your child's understanding
You can check your child's understanding of simple science concepts by asking questions like, "It is cold today. Which clothes should you put on? What will happen when I throw this ball?"

CONTENTS

Things that move

Things can move quickly or slowly, forward or backward, or even around and around!

Ben and Sam move fast, but Jane is too slow!

Beep! Beep! Beep!

I can move forward ...

... and backward.

You can move in lots of different ways. Can you make ...

... tiny steps?

... giant steps?

up and down

How do these things move?

around and around

Did you know?

The sleek cheetah is the fastest animal on Earth.

4

Wheels are round.

Wheels help things move smoothly and easily.

This wheelbarrow is easy to move but ...

... this one isn't. Can you see what's missing?

All these things have wheels.

bicycle

toy tractor

skateboard

The fire engine will move quickly down this slope ...

... but faster down this slope. Do you know why?

Try this!

Make a pull-along wagon

1. Trace around a cup on cardboard to make four wheels. Cut them out.

2. Push two pencils through two wheels. Attach them with modeling clay.

3. Make four holes in a small box. Push pencils into the holes.

4. Attach wheels to the other end of the pencils with modeling clay. Tie string to one end.

Push and pull

When you push or pull, you can make something move.

pushing a go-cart

Pull, Emma ...

How do you make ...

... a toy dog move?

Pull hard, Emma and Sam ...

... a scooter move?

Pull harder, Emma, Sam and Anna ...

Hooray! They've done it.

Try this!

Magic bucket

Pour a little water into a bucket. Swing it around and around, with a straight arm.

The rush of air will push the water into the the bucket, and it won't fall out!

Ted has to push and pull with his legs to make the swing move.

Wheee! This is fun!

Push and pull some clay to make a fierce dragon!

When you get dressed, you ...

... pull up your socks

... push your feet into your shoes

... push your hands into your gloves

... pull on a t-shirt

... pull down your hat

Pull your lips and push out your tongue. What a funny face!

7

Floating and sinking

Some things, like boats and ducks, float on water. Other things sink.

Diving Bear will find out which things sink.

Try this!

Make a sail boat

1. Cut a triangular sail from cardboard. Glue a straw to its back.

2. Fold the end of the sail over the straw. Tape the flap to the back of the sail.

3. Press a ball of modeling clay into the bottom of a plastic bowl.

4. Push the straw into the modeling clay.

A sailboat floats.

Ducks float on water...

... and so does Ted's rubber inner tube.

Diving Bear finds things that sink ...

... sinking gold coins

... an anchor

... a pirate's sunken treasure chest

... sand, pebbles and shells

Drop lots of different things into some water. Which ones float? Which ones sink? You are doing an investigation.

pencils

socks

wooden blocks

Make a chart on a sheet of paper.

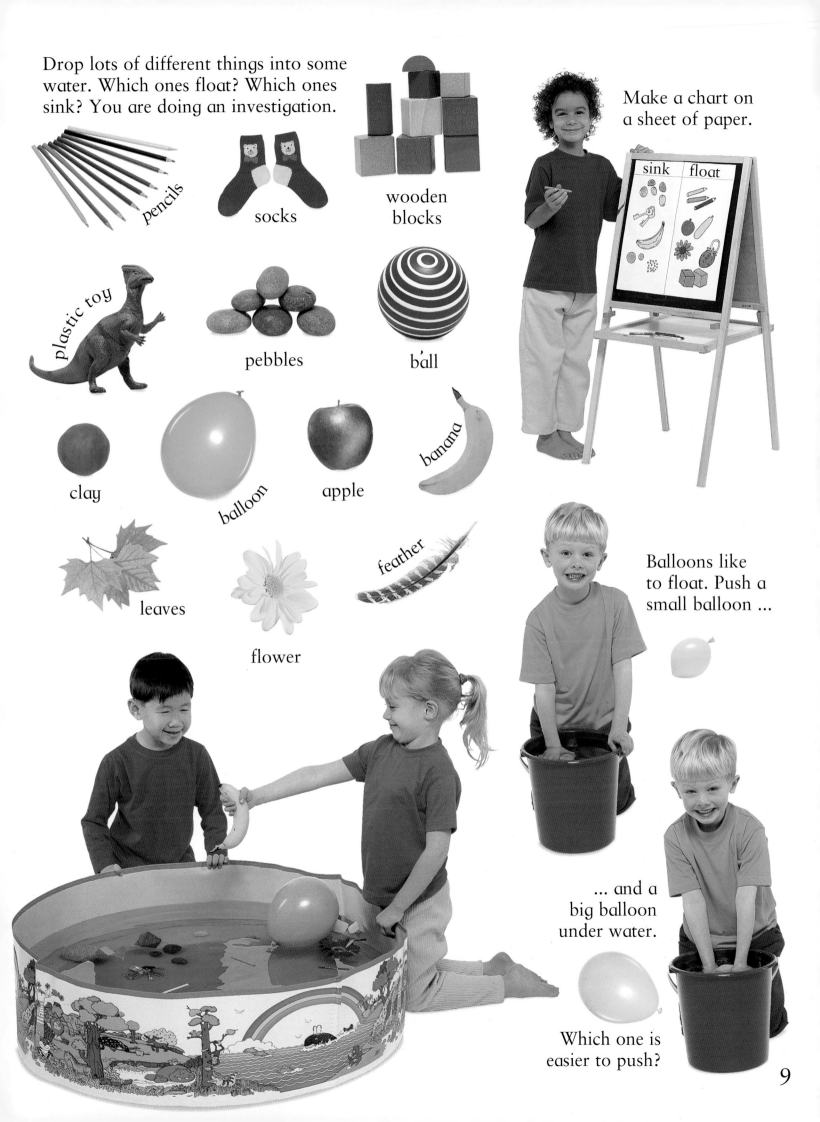

sink | float

plastic toy

pebbles

ball

clay

balloon

apple

banana

leaves

flower

feather

Balloons like to float. Push a small balloon ...

... and a big balloon under water.

Which one is easier to push?

9

Air and wind

You can't see air, but it's all around you.
There is even air inside your body!

Have you ever ...

... blown
bubbles full
of air?

... pumped air
into a balloon?

The air in this
bag came from
John's lungs.

... blown out
birthday
candles?

... seen
bubbles
of air in a
fizzy drink?

When air moves, it can
make other things move.
Wind is moving air.

On a windy day ...

... a windsock
fills with air

... hair gets
blown around

... a kite flies

... leaves
flutter

Try this!

Make a "flying" balloon

1. Thread a straw onto a long piece of string.

2. Inflate a long balloon. Stop the air from escaping with a clamp.

3. Tape the straw to the balloon.

4. Ask friends to hold the ends of the string. Release the clamp. The balloon will "fly"!

arm floats

These things have air inside them:

soccer ball

balloons

bouncing ball

Pretend to be the wind. Blow on the sails to make the boats move.

An umbrella can be turned inside-out by the wind.

Gravity

Things fall to the ground because of an invisible force called gravity.

Going up is hard work ...

... but sliding down is easy!

Wheee!

What goes up ... must come down!

When you jump into the air ...

... gravity pulls you down.

A Slinky slinks down.

These toys work because of gravity.

The marble rolls down the marble run.

Gravity pulls the woodpecker down the stick.

tap tap

Did you know?

There is no gravity in space. If you threw a ball into space it would float away from you.

What happens if Peter stops juggling?

Orange juice!

Which of these things falls the fastest and reaches the ground first?

A piece of paper or, ...

... a ball of paper?

Two identical balls?

A feather or ...

... a plastic toy?

Will the ball roll up or down the slope?

Try this!

Make a gravity painting

1. Pour spoonfuls of tempera paint onto a piece of cardboard.

2. Tilt the cardboard side to side, and backward and forward. The paint will run and make patterns.

13

Balance

If something is balanced,
it will not topple over.

Watch Freddy Frog
and his friends balance ...

One of these towers
will fall over because
it is not balanced.

Do you know
which one?

... a spinning
plate

... two cherry cupcakes

... on one
leg with
eyes shut

... on a drum

... on stepping stones

... on a tightrope

Try this!

Make a stand-up person

1. Fold a large rectangular piece of cardboard in half.

2. Draw a person on it. Make sure the top of the head is along the fold.

3. Cut it out, but do not cut along the fold.

4. Draw a face. Make your stand-up person stand up and balance.

Which of these is balanced?

The ice cream cone or ...

... the wizard's hat?

This chair ...

... or this one?

This tower ...

... or this one?

Spin around in a large, open space to make yourself dizzy.

When you stop, is it hard to keep your balance?

This see-saw ...

... or this see-saw?

15

Hot and cold

Hot and cold things feel different to touch. Some things change when they are heated up or cooled down.

To make yourself warm ...

phew!

You sweat when you're hot.

brrr!

You shiver when you're cold.

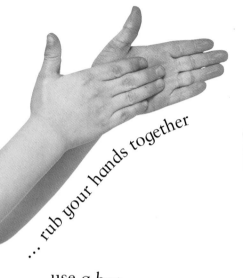

... rub your hands together

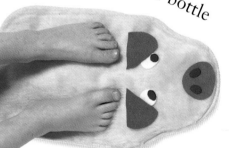

... use a hot water bottle

... wear lots of layers

Stay cool with a breeze from a fan.

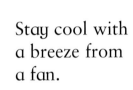

Some food has to be kept cold in a refrigerator.

Yuck, warm sour milk!

Try this!

Crunchy chocolate candies

1. Wash your hands. Break a 1-pound chocolate bar into pieces. Ask a grown-up to help you melt it.

2. Mix the melted chocolate with 2 cups of crunchy cereal.

3. Spoon it into cupcake papers. Place them in the refrigerator to get hard.

16

Here are some things that change when heated or cooled. Be careful! Hot things can burn you.

Cheese melts ...

... when it is cooked.

Chocolate melts in your warm fingers.

Frozen water is solid.

Melted ice is liquid.

Chocolate cake batter becomes ... cooked cake.

Butter ... melts on hot toast.

Yummy ice cream ...

Cook a raw egg to make ... a scrambled egg ... or a fried egg.

... melts when it gets warm.

Your body

Your body has lots of different parts. You can see some parts, but others are hidden under the skin.

Hard nails protect your fingertips.

head

fingers

arm

hair

hand

elbow

chest

Can you feel your hard skull ...

waist

... and the bones in your knees?

bottom

hip

leg

knee

ankle

foot

toes

There are lots of bones in your feet.

The bottom of your ear and the tip of your nose are soft.

18

Under your skin are muscles and bones. They help you to ...

... climb

... eat

... paint

... run

What else can you do with your body?

Your skin can make a ...

... funny face.

Your heart pumps blood around your body.

thump

thump

Have you ever listened to your heart?

You go to sleep at night because your body needs to rest.

Did you know?

Your brain tells your body what to do. It is inside your head. Your brain weighs about the same as 12 apples.

19

Growing

All living things grow and get bigger. To grow, they need food, water and sunlight.

Look at how much Fred has grown!

big girl

little girl

baby girl

Fluffy chicks grow up to be chickens.

Puppies grow up to be dogs.

This hairy caterpillar goes to sleep in a cocoon and changes into a butterfly.

When some animals grow, they change completely!

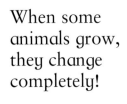

20

Try this!

Growing a bean seed

1. Get some bean seeds.

2. Push the seeds into some soil in a pot.

3. Put the pot in a sunny spot and water each day.

4. Watch your bean seeds grow.

You wouldn't eat soil for dinner, but growing plants get their food from soil.

Look at how a hyacinth plant grows. Where are its roots?

It starts as a bulb.

It then grows a leafy stem.

Leaves and a flower bud grow.

Leaves grow taller and the flower opens.

Frogs lay eggs called spawn. Tadpoles hatch from eggs and grow into frogs. Croak!

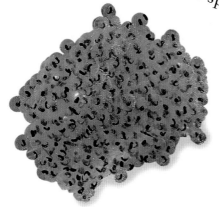

21

Touching and feeling

You feel with your skin. You can learn about things by the way they feel.

strawberry

orange

banana

Ouch!

A prickly holly bush.

What do these fruits feel like?

pineapple

mango

grapes

Your sense of touch warns you of danger.

We like to wear things that feel nice. Which of these things would you wear?

A soft sweater or ...

... an itchy one?

Try this!

A feely picture

1. Glue felt, tinfoil and sandpaper onto cardboard.

2. Use cotton-balls, a sponge, cardboard and shells to make a beach scene.

Fluffy gray slippers or ...

... scrub brush slippers?

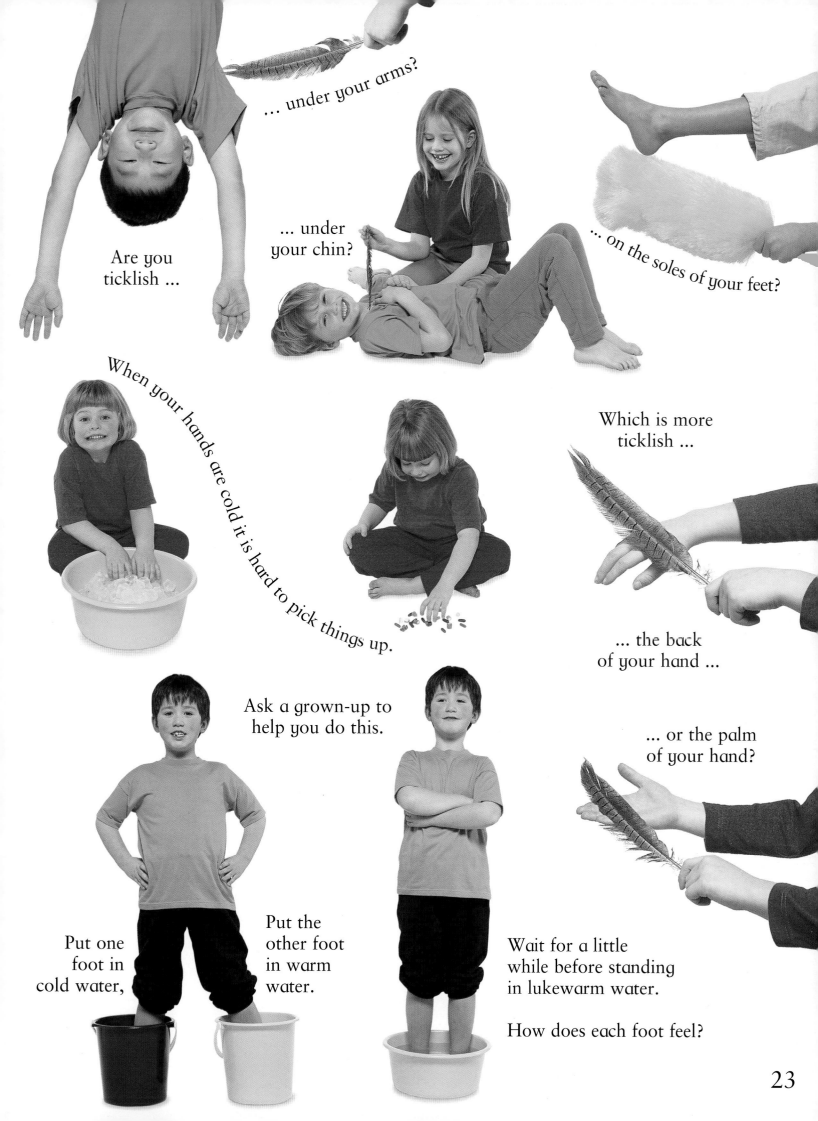

... under your arms?

Are you ticklish ...

... under your chin?

... on the soles of your feet?

When your hands are cold it is hard to pick things up.

Which is more ticklish ...

... the back of your hand ...

Ask a grown-up to help you do this.

... or the palm of your hand?

Put one foot in cold water,

Put the other foot in warm water.

Wait for a little while before standing in lukewarm water.

How does each foot feel?

23

Sound and hearing

Our ears help us to hear sounds.
Sounds are made by vibrations moving through the air.

I can hear you.

I can hear you too.

What a lot of noise!

ring ring

What sounds do these noisy things make?

jingle jingle

honk! honk! honk!

bang! crash!

toot toot

Did you know?

Elephants have excellent hearing. They can hear one another from at least 2½ miles away!

Try this!

Sshh! A whispering game

1. Sit your friends in a circle. Make up a silly rhyme.

2. Whisper it to the friend sitting next to you.

3. Keep going around the circle until the whisper gets back to you. Is your silly rhyme still the same?

Record yourself talking and singing, then play it back.

Does it sound like you?

Your voice will travel through this tube.

Sounds can change. Try shouting into a bucket.

Your tongue helps you make sounds.

Does your voice sound different?

Sing with your tongue like this ... ... and then like this.

Making music

When air is squashed or moved it makes a noise. Different things are used to squash and move air to make music.

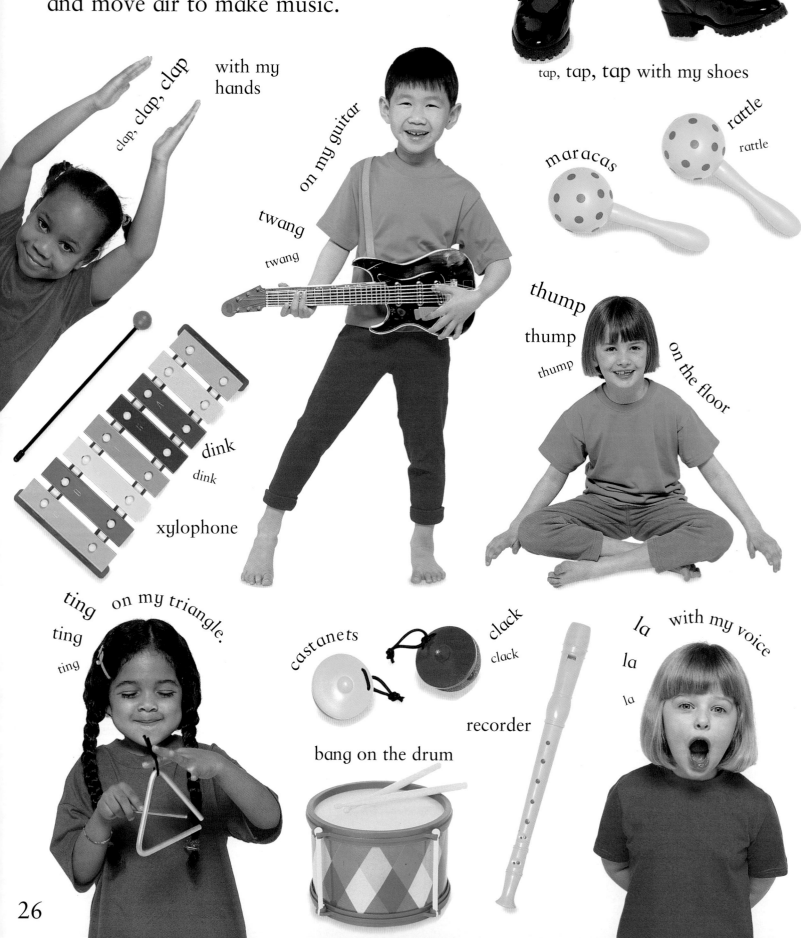

tap, tap, tap with my shoes

clap, clap, clap with my hands

on my guitar

twang
twang

rattle
rattle

maracas

thump
thump
thump

on the floor

dink
dink

xylophone

ting on my triangle.
ting
ting

castanets

clack
clack

la with my voice
la
la

recorder

bang on the drum

26

You can make music
using things in your home.
You can make ...

... a loud
sound

... low sounds

...or high sounds

... a quiet
sound

... wind
sounds

... lots of
different
clinking
sounds

... soft rustling noises

...very loud noises

Try this!

Make a shaker

1. Get some
dried lentils
or beans.

2. Put them in
a plastic cup.

3. Place a cup
on top. Attach
them with tape.

4. Shake
it up and
down and
side to side
to make sounds.

Color

Different colors are all around us. Some colors are dark, some are light.

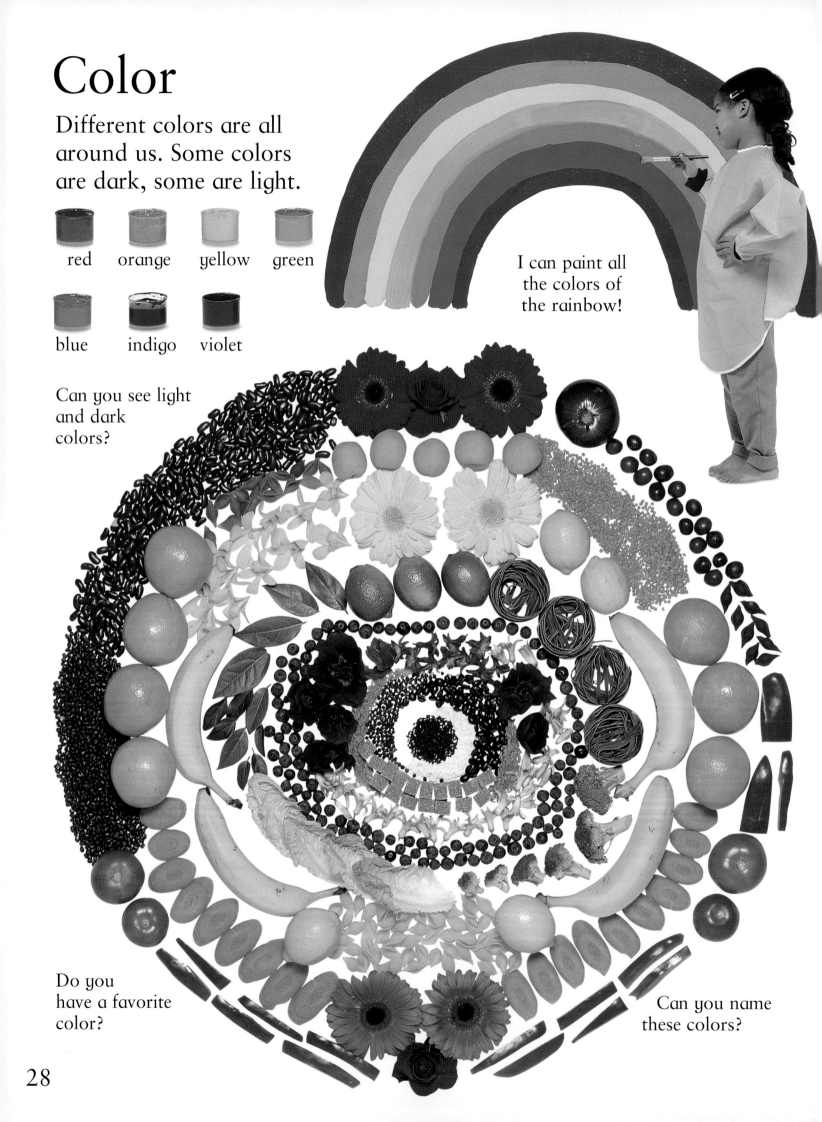

red   orange   yellow   green

blue   indigo   violet

I can paint all the colors of the rainbow!

Can you see light and dark colors?

Do you have a favorite color?

Can you name these colors?

Use cellophane to make crazy colored glasses. What happens to the colors around you?

You can make lots of different colors by mixing red, yellow and blue.

 +  =

Red and yellow make orange.

Red and blue make purple.

 +  =

Blue and yellow make green.

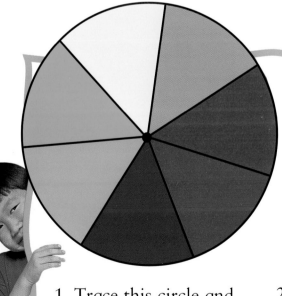

Try this!

Make a magic wheel

3. Spin the wheel fast. What color is it?

1. Trace this circle and lines onto tracing paper. Transfer the tracing to a piece of white cardboard.

2. Cut out the circle. Color it in exactly as shown. Push a pencil through the center.

Question and answer game

Answer the questions and then make your way through the maze to see if your answers are correct. Give yourself a point for every question you get right.

START

What happens if the popsicle gets warm?

John goes down the slide.

A dog.

It melts.

What does a puppy grow into?

What happens next?

What happens when Sam blows on the candles?

The candles will go out.

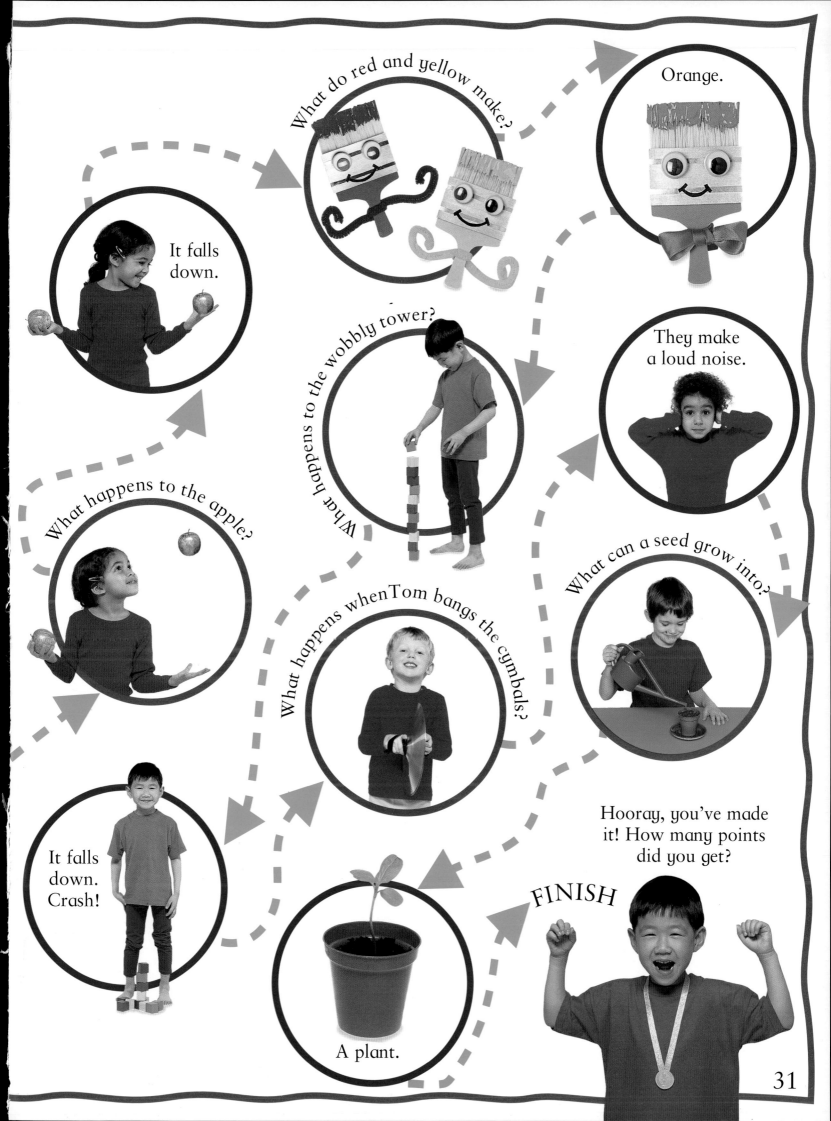

What do red and yellow make?

Orange.

It falls down.

What happens to the wobbly tower?

They make a loud noise.

What happens to the apple?

What can a seed grow into?

What happens when Tom bangs the cymbals?

It falls down. Crash!

Hooray, you've made it! How many points did you get?

FINISH

A plant.

This edition published by Lorenz Books
27 West 20th Street, New York, NY 10011

LORENZ BOOKS are available for bulk purchase for
sales promotion and for premium use.
For details, write or call the sales director, Lorenz Books,
27 West 20th Street, New York,
NY 10011; (800)354-9657.

Lorenz Books is an imprint of Anness Publishing Inc.

All rights reserved. No part of this publication may be reproduced, stored in a retrieval
system, or transmitted in any way or by any means, electronic, mechanical,
photocopying, recording or otherwise, without the prior written permission of the
copyright holder.

ISBN 1 85967 832 7

Publisher: Joanna Lorenz
Managing Editor, Children's Books: Sue Grabham
Project Manager: Lyn Coutts
Educational Consultant: Sharon Whittingham B.Ed.
Design: Louise Millar, Mike Leaman
Photography: John Freeman
Head Stylist: Melanie Williams
Stylist: Ken Campbell

The Publishers would like to thank the following children for modeling in this book:
Irene Agu, Rosie Anness, Harriet Bartholomew, Jonathon Bartholomew, Daisy
Bartlett, Kitty Bartlett, Ambika Berczuk, April Cain, Callum Collins, Matthew
Ferguson, Luke Fry, Safari George, Saffron George, Zaafir Ghany, Billy Haggans,
Miriam Nadia Halgane, Maddison Harrington, Faye Harrison, Kadeem Johnson,
Zamour Johnson, Archie-Leigh Jones, Sumaya Khassal, Cleo Kinder, Holly Matthews,
Jack Matthews, Rebekah Murrell, Lucie Ozanne-Martin, Philip Quach,
Tom Rawlings, Ashley Read, Olivia Risveglia and Georgina Thomas.
Picture credits: 4 BR Clem Haagner; 13 TL Science Photo Library; 20 CL Jane
Burton; 20 CR and C Jane Ellis; 20 BL, C and BR Papillio Photographic; 21 BL and
BR Stephen Dalton, NHPA; 21 BC Jane Burton.

Printed and bound in Singapore
© Anness Publishing Limited 1998
Updated © 1999

1 3 5 7 9 10 8 6 4 2